Enjoying The Journey RV Travel Log

Traveling Nova Scotia

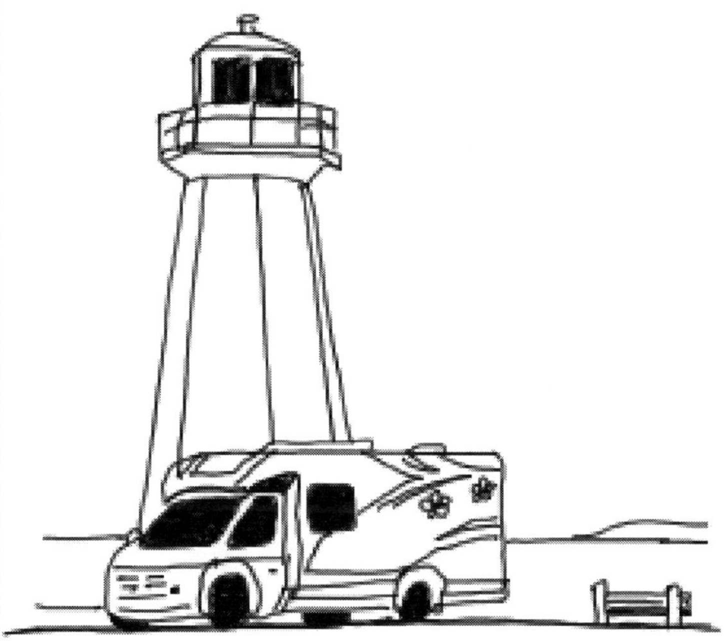

This Book Belongs to

____

Year of camping memories

____

NOVA SCOTIA BEACHES

WHAT ONES HAVE YOU VISITED

BEACHES	✓
THE HAWK BEACH	○
PONDVILLE BEACH	○
CRESCENT BEACH	○
INDIAN BEACH	○
CARTER'S BEACH	○
INGONISH BEACH	○
CARIBOU/MUNROES BEACH	○
CHETICAMP ISLAND BEACH	○
DOLLAR LAKE BEACH	○
ELLENWOOD LAKE BEACH	○
BLACK BROOK BEACH	○
MC CORMACKS BEACH	○
WEST MABOU BEACH	○
CRYSTAL CRESCENT BEACH	○
SANDY COVE BEACH	○
RISSERS BEACH	○
CONRADS BEACH	○
HIRTLE BEACH	○
NORTHPOINT BEACH	○
MAVILLETTE BEACH	○
LA BLOC BEACH	○
CLEVELAND BEACH	○
THOMAS RADDALL BEACH	○
POMQUET BEACH	○
MARTINIQUE BEACH	○
RAINBOW HAVEN BEACH	○
BLUE SEA BEACH	○
WATERSIDE BEACH	○
BAYSWATER BEACH	○
BEACH MEADOWS BEACH	○
LAWRENCETOWN BEACH	○
MELMERBY BEACH	○
POINT MICHAUD BEACH	○
SUMMERVILLE BEACH	○
KINGSBURG BEACH	○
QUEENSLAND BEACH	○
KENNINGTON COVE BEACH	○
ROSEWAY BEACH	○
BLUE BEACH	○
CLAM HARBOUR BEACH	○
HEATHER BEACH	○
PORT HOOD BEACH	○
RUSHTONS BEACH	○

NOVA SCOTIA PROVINCIAL & NATIONAL CAMPGROUNDS

WHAT ONES HAVE YOU VISITED

CAMPGROUND ✓

- AMHERST SHORE ○
- BATTERY ○
- BLOMIDON ○
- BOYLSTON ○
- CAPE CHIGNECTO -WALK IN ○
- CARIBOU MUNROES ○
- DOLLAR LAKE ○
- ELLENWOOD LAKE ○
- FIVE ISLANDS ○
- GRAVES ISLAND ○
- LAURIE ○
- MIRA RIVER ○
- PORTERS LAKE ○
- RISSERS BEACH ○
- SALSMAN ○
- SMILEYS ○
- THE ISLANDS ○
- THOMAS RADDALL ○
- VALLEY VIEW ○
- WHYCOCOMAGH ○

CAPE BRETON HIGHLANDS

- BROAD COVE ○
- CAP- ROUGE MKWESAQTUK ○
- CHETICAMP ○
- INGONIGH BEACH ○
- FIGHING COVE -WALK IN ○

KEJIMKUJIK

- JEREMY'S BAY ○

NOTES

NOVA SCOTIA PRIVATE CAMPGROUNDS

WHAT ONES HAVE YOU VISITED

CAMPGROUND	✓	KEEP FILLING IN MORE CAMPGROUNDS	
WHALE OF A TIME	○	NORSE COVE	○
	○		○
	○		○
MCLEODS BEACH	○	KING NEPTUNE	○
	○		○
	○		○
MURPHY'S ON THE WATER	○	HUBBARDS BEACH	○
	○		○
	○		○
YOGI BEAR JELLYSTONE	○	SEAFOAM	○
	○		○
	○		○
BIRCHWOOD	○	SUNSET SANDS	○
	○		○
	○		○
OAKHILL PINES	○	DUNROMIN	○
	○		○
ARM OF GOLD	○	HIDE AWAY	○

NOVA SCOTIA PRIVATE CAMPGROUNDS

WHAT ONES HAVE YOU VISITED

CAMPGROUND ✓ KEEP FILLING IN MORE CAMPGROUNDS

- KOA HALIFAX WEST
- COVE OCEANFRONT
- LINWOOD HARBOUR
- HYCLASS OCEAN
- WHALE COVE
- LUNENBURG RV PARK
- BRIDGETOWN
- BRAS D'OR LAKES
- GATEWAY
- E&F WEBBER
- GLOOSCAP
- WAYSIDE
- KOA NORTH SYDNEY
- BADDECK CABOT TRAIL

BIKING & HIKING TRAILS I WANT TO VISIT THIS YEAR

TRAILS		✓ KEEP FILLING IN MORE	
SKYLINE TRAIL	○	POINT PLEASANT PARK TRAILS	○
	○		○
CAPE CHIGNECTO LOOP TRAIL	○	CAPE SPLIT TRAIL	○
	○		○
RUM RUNNERS TRAIL	○	SALT MARSH TRAIL	○
	○		○
JITNEY TRAIL	○	HARVEST MOON TRAILWAY	○
	○		○
SHORT LINE TRAIL	○	CELTIC SHORES COASTAL TRAIL	○

BIKING & HIKING TRAILS I WANT TO VISIT THIS YEAR

TRAILS ✓ KEEP FILLING IN MORE

PLACES I WANT TO VISIT THIS YEAR

ATTRACTIONS	✓	KEEP FILLING IN MORE	
PEGGY'S COVE	○	MINERS MUSEUM	○
	○		○
OAKLAND FARN ZOO	○	BALANCING ROCK	○
	○		○
CITADEL HILL	○	SHUBENACADIE WILDLIFE PARK	○
	○		○
JOGGINS FOSSIL CLIFFS	○	FORTRESS OF LOUISBOURG	○
	○		○
THE CABOT TRAIL	○	VICTORIA PARK	○

PLACES I WANT TO VISIT THIS YEAR

ATTRACTIONS ✓ KEEP FILLING IN MORE

MY CAMPING TRAVEL PLAN

Date: --------------

TRAVEL DIARY

S S M T W T F

Date:

Travel from :

Travel to :

Travel To-do List

Today's Travel Info

BEGINING MILEAGE

ENDING MILEAGE

MILES TRAVELLED

COST

FUEL

TRAVEL TIME

WEATHER

TEMPERATURE

Today's Expenses

Note:

CAMPGROUND DETAILS

Date: ______________

TRAVEL ITINERARY

S S M T W T F

AMENITIES	✓
WATER	○
ELECTRIC	○
SEWER	○
BACK IN	○
PULL THROUGH	○
SUN	○
SHADE	○
LEVEL	○
SLOPE	○
PAVED	○
PICNIC TABLE	○
FIRE PIT	○
WIFI	○
STORE	○
POOL	○
RESTROOMS	○
CLEAN	○
PET FRIENDLY	○
KID FRIENDLY	○

ACCOMODATION

Campground Name

Location:

Phone #

Site #

Cost $

# of Days staying

Site I Would Stay next time

____

Cell service ______________________

Notes ______________________

____

☆☆☆☆☆ Rating

PRIVACY	○
QUITE	○
NOISY	○
GRASS	○
GRAVEL	○

PLACES TO VISIT

THINGS TO DO

PLACES TO SEE

TRAILS, HIKING & BIKING

FOOD, DINING &RESTAURANTS

THINGS TO DO NEXT TIME

PEOPLE WE MET

HIGHLIGHTS

TRAVEL JOURNAL

MEMORIES AND PHOTOS

This Trip was...

MY CAMPING TRAVEL PLAN

Date: ______________

TRAVEL DIARY

S S M T W T F

Date:

Travel from :

Travel to :

Travel To-do List

Today's Travel Info

BEGINING MILEAGE

ENDING MILEAGE

MILES TRAVELLED

COST

FUEL

TRAVEL TIME

WEATHER

TEMPERATURE

Note:

Today's Expenses

CAMPGROUND DETAILS

TRAVEL ITINERARY

Date: ______________

S S M T W T F

AMENITIES	✓
WATER	○
ELECTRIC	○
SEWER	○
BACK IN	○
PULL THROUGH	○
SUN	○
SHADE	○
LEVEL	○
SLOPE	○
PAVED	○
PICNIC TABLE	○
FIRE PIT	○
WIFI	○
STORE	○
POOL	○
RESTROOMS	○
CLEAN	○
PET FRIENDLY	○
KID FRIENDLY	○

ACCOMODATION

Campground Name

Location:

Phone #

Site #

Cost $

# of Days staying

Site I Would Stay next time

____

Cell service ____________________

Notes ________________________

____

☆☆☆☆☆ Rating

PRIVACY	○
QUITE	○
NOISY	○
GRASS	○
GRAVEL	○

PLACES TO VISIT

THINGS TO DO

PLACES TO SEE

TRAILS, HIKING & BIKING

FOOD, DINING &RESTAURANTS

THINGS TO DO NEXT TIME

PEOPLE WE MET

HIGHLIGHTS

TRAVEL JOURNAL

MEMORIES AND PHOTOS

This Trip was...

MY CAMPING TRAVEL PLAN

Date: --------------

TRAVEL DIARY

S S M T W T F

Date:

Travel from :

Travel to :

Travel To-do List

Today's Expenses

Today's Travel Info

BEGINING MILEAGE	
ENDING MILEAGE	
MILES TRAVELLED	
COST	
FUEL	
TRAVEL TIME	
WEATHER	
TEMPERATURE	

Note:

CAMPGROUND DETAILS

TRAVEL ITINERARY

Date: ______________

S S M T W T F

AMENITIES	✓
WATER	○
ELECTRIC	○
SEWER	○
BACK IN	○
PULL THROUGH	○
SUN	○
SHADE	○
LEVEL	○
SLOPE	○
PAVED	○
PICNIC TABLE	○
FIRE PIT	○
WIFI	○
STORE	○
POOL	○
RESTROOMS	○
CLEAN	○
PET FRIENDLY	○
KID FRIENDLY	○

ACCOMODATION

Campground Name

Location:

Phone #

Site #

Cost $

# of Days staying

Site I Would Stay next time

____

Cell service ______________________

Notes ______________________

____

☆☆☆☆☆ Rating

PRIVACY	○
QUITE	○
NOISY	○
GRASS	○
GRAVEL	○

PLACES TO VISIT

THINGS TO DO

PLACES TO SEE

TRAILS, HIKING & BIKING

FOOD, DINING &RESTAURANTS

THINGS TO DO NEXT TIME

PEOPLE WE MET

HIGHLIGHTS

TRAVEL JOURNAL

MEMORIES AND PHOTOS

This Trip was...

MY CAMPING TRAVEL PLAN

Date: --------------

TRAVEL DIARY

S S M T W T F

Date:

Travel from :

Travel to :

Travel To-do List

Today's Expenses

Today's Travel Info

BEGINING MILEAGE

ENDING MILEAGE

MILES TRAVELLED

COST

FUEL

TRAVEL TIME

WEATHER

TEMPERATURE

Note:

CAMPGROUND DETAILS

Date: --------------

TRAVEL ITINERARY

S S M T W T F

AMENITIES	✓
WATER	○
ELECTRIC	○
SEWER	○
BACK IN	○
PULL THROUGH	○
SUN	○
SHADE	○
LEVEL	○
SLOPE	○
PAVED	○
PICNIC TABLE	○
FIRE PIT	○
WIFI	○
STORE	○
POOL	○
RESTROOMS	○
CLEAN	○
PET FRIENDLY	○
KID FRIENDLY	○

ACCOMODATION

Campground Name

Location:

Phone #

Site #

Cost $

# of Days staying

Site I Would Stay next time

____

Cell service ______________________

Notes ______________________

____

☆☆☆☆☆ Rating

PRIVACY	○
QUITE	○
NOISY	○
GRASS	○
GRAVEL	○

PLACES TO VISIT

THINGS TO DO

PLACES TO SEE

TRAILS, HIKING & BIKING

FOOD, DINING &RESTAURANTS

THINGS TO DO NEXT TIME

PEOPLE WE MET

HIGHLIGHTS

TRAVEL JOURNAL

MEMORIES AND PHOTOS

This Trip was...

MY CAMPING TRAVEL PLAN

Date: --------------

TRAVEL DIARY

S S M T W T F

Date:

Travel from :

Travel to :

Travel To-do List

Today's Expenses

Today's Travel Info

BEGINING MILEAGE

ENDING MILEAGE

MILES TRAVELLED

COST

FUEL

TRAVEL TIME

WEATHER

TEMPERATURE

Note:

CAMPGROUND DETAILS

TRAVEL ITINERARY

Date: ______________

S S M T W T F

AMENITIES	✔
WATER	○
ELECTRIC	○
SEWER	○
BACK IN	○
PULL THROUGH	○
SUN	○
SHADE	○
LEVEL	○
SLOPE	○
PAVED	○
PICNIC TABLE	○
FIRE PIT	○
WIFI	○
STORE	○
POOL	○
RESTROOMS	○
CLEAN	○
PET FRIENDLY	○
KID FRIENDLY	○

ACCOMODATION

Campground Name

Location:

Phone #

Site #

Cost $

# of Days staying

Site I Would Stay next time

____

Cell service ____________________

Notes ________________________

____

☆☆☆☆☆ Rating

PRIVACY	○
QUITE	○
NOISY	○
GRASS	○
GRAVEL	○

PLACES TO VISIT

THINGS TO DO

PLACES TO SEE

TRAILS, HIKING & BIKING

FOOD, DINING &RESTAURANTS

THINGS TO DO NEXT TIME

PEOPLE WE MET

HIGHLIGHTS

TRAVEL JOURNAL

MEMORIES AND PHOTOS

This Trip was...

MY CAMPING TRAVEL PLAN

Date: ---------------

TRAVEL DIARY

S S M T W T F

Date:

Travel from :

Travel to :

Travel To-do List

Today's Expenses

Today's Travel Info

BEGINING MILEAGE	
ENDING MILEAGE	
MILES TRAVELLED	
COST	
FUEL	
TRAVEL TIME	
WEATHER	
TEMPERATURE	

Note:

CAMPGROUND DETAILS

TRAVEL ITINERARY

Date: ______________

S S M T W T F

AMENITIES	✓
WATER	○
ELECTRIC	○
SEWER	○
BACK IN	○
PULL THROUGH	○
SUN	○
SHADE	○
LEVEL	○
SLOPE	○
PAVED	○
PICNIC TABLE	○
FIRE PIT	○
WIFI	○
STORE	○
POOL	○
RESTROOMS	○
CLEAN	○
PET FRIENDLY	○
KID FRIENDLY	○

ACCOMODATION

Campground Name

Location:

Phone #

Site #

Cost $

# of Days staying

Site I Would Stay next time

____

Cell service ______________________

Notes ______________________

____

☆☆☆☆☆ Rating

PRIVACY	○
QUITE	○
NOISY	○
GRASS	○
GRAVEL	○

PLACES TO VISIT

THINGS TO DO

PLACES TO SEE

TRAILS, HIKING & BIKING

FOOD, DINING &RESTAURANTS

THINGS TO DO NEXT TIME

PEOPLE WE MET

HIGHLIGHTS

TRAVEL JOURNAL

MEMORIES AND PHOTOS

This Trip was...

MY CAMPING TRAVEL PLAN

Date: --------------

TRAVEL DIARY

S S M T W T F

Date:

Travel from :

Travel to :

Travel To-do List

Today's Travel Info

BEGINING MILEAGE

ENDING MILEAGE

MILES TRAVELLED

COST

FUEL

TRAVEL TIME

WEATHER

TEMPERATURE

Note:

Today's Expenses

CAMPGROUND DETAILS

TRAVEL ITINERARY

Date: ______________

S S M T W T F

AMENITIES	✔
WATER	○
ELECTRIC	○
SEWER	○
BACK IN	○
PULL THROUGH	○
SUN	○
SHADE	○
LEVEL	○
SLOPE	○
PAVED	○
PICNIC TABLE	○
FIRE PIT	○
WIFI	○
STORE	○
POOL	○
RESTROOMS	○
CLEAN	○
PET FRIENDLY	○
KID FRIENDLY	○

ACCOMODATION

Campground Name

Location:

Phone #

Site #

Cost $

# of Days staying

Site I Would Stay next time

____

Cell service ____________________

Notes ____________________

____

☆☆☆☆☆ Rating

PRIVACY	○
QUITE	○
NOISY	○
GRASS	○
GRAVEL	○

PLACES TO VISIT

THINGS TO DO

PLACES TO SEE

TRAILS, HIKING & BIKING

FOOD, DINING &RESTAURANTS

THINGS TO DO NEXT TIME

PEOPLE WE MET

HIGHLIGHTS

TRAVEL JOURNAL

MEMORIES AND PHOTOS

This Trip was...

MY CAMPING TRAVEL PLAN

Date: --------------

TRAVEL DIARY

S S M T W T F

Date:

Travel from :

Travel to :

Travel To-do List

Today's Expenses

Today's Travel Info

BEGINING MILEAGE

ENDING MILEAGE

MILES TRAVELLED

COST

FUEL

TRAVEL TIME

WEATHER

TEMPERATURE

Note:

CAMPGROUND DETAILS

Date: _____________

TRAVEL ITINERARY

S S M T W T F

AMENITIES	✓
WATER	○
ELECTRIC	○
SEWER	○
BACK IN	○
PULL THROUGH	○
SUN	○
SHADE	○
LEVEL	○
SLOPE	○
PAVED	○
PICNIC TABLE	○
FIRE PIT	○
WIFI	○
STORE	○
POOL	○
RESTROOMS	○
CLEAN	○
PET FRIENDLY	○
KID FRIENDLY	○

ACCOMODATION

Campground Name

Location:

Phone #

Site #

Cost $

# of Days staying

Site I Would Stay next time

____

Cell service _______________

Notes _______________

____

☆☆☆☆☆ Rating

PRIVACY	○
QUITE	○
NOISY	○
GRASS	○
GRAVEL	○

PLACES TO VISIT

THINGS TO DO

PLACES TO SEE

TRAILS, HIKING & BIKING

FOOD, DINING &RESTAURANTS

THINGS TO DO NEXT TIME

PEOPLE WE MET

HIGHLIGHTS

TRAVEL JOURNAL

MEMORIES AND PHOTOS

This Trip was...

MY CAMPING TRAVEL PLAN

Date: _____________

TRAVEL DIARY

S S M T W T F

Date:

Travel from :

Travel to :

Travel To-do List

Today's Expenses

Today's Travel Info

BEGINING MILEAGE

ENDING MILEAGE

MILES TRAVELLED

COST

FUEL

TRAVEL TIME

WEATHER

TEMPERATURE

Note:

CAMPGROUND DETAILS

Date: _____________

TRAVEL ITINERARY

S S M T W T F

AMENITIES	✔
WATER	○
ELECTRIC	○
SEWER	○
BACK IN	○
PULL THROUGH	○
SUN	○
SHADE	○
LEVEL	○
SLOPE	○
PAVED	○
PICNIC TABLE	○
FIRE PIT	○
WIFI	○
STORE	○
POOL	○
RESTROOMS	○
CLEAN	○
PET FRIENDLY	○
KID FRIENDLY	○

ACCOMODATION

Campground Name

Location:

Phone #

Site #

Cost $

# of Days staying

Site I Would Stay next time

____

Cell service ____________________

Notes ____________________

____

☆☆☆☆☆ Rating

PRIVACY	○
QUITE	○
NOISY	○
GRASS	○
GRAVEL	○

PLACES TO VISIT

THINGS TO DO

PLACES TO SEE

TRAILS, HIKING & BIKING

FOOD, DINING &RESTAURANTS

THINGS TO DO NEXT TIME

PEOPLE WE MET

HIGHLIGHTS

TRAVEL JOURNAL

MEMORIES AND PHOTOS

This Trip was...

MY CAMPING TRAVEL PLAN

Date: --------------

TRAVEL DIARY

S S M T W T F

Date:

Travel from :

Travel to :

Travel To-do List

Today's Expenses

Today's Travel Info

BEGINING MILEAGE

ENDING MILEAGE

MILES TRAVELLED

COST

FUEL

TRAVEL TIME

WEATHER

TEMPERATURE

Note:

CAMPGROUND DETAILS

TRAVEL ITINERARY

Date: ______________

S S M T W T F

AMENITIES	✓
WATER	○
ELECTRIC	○
SEWER	○
BACK IN	○
PULL THROUGH	○
SUN	○
SHADE	○
LEVEL	○
SLOPE	○
PAVED	○
PICNIC TABLE	○
FIRE PIT	○
WIFI	○
STORE	○
POOL	○
RESTROOMS	○
CLEAN	○
PET FRIENDLY	○
KID FRIENDLY	○

ACCOMODATION

Campground Name

Location:

Phone #

Site #

Cost $

# of Days staying

Site I Would Stay next time

____

Cell service ____________________

Notes ____________________

____

☆☆☆☆☆ Rating

PRIVACY	○
QUITE	○
NOISY	○
GRASS	○
GRAVEL	○

PLACES TO VISIT

THINGS TO DO

PLACES TO SEE

TRAILS, HIKING & BIKING

FOOD, DINING &RESTAURANTS

THINGS TO DO NEXT TIME

PEOPLE WE MET

HIGHLIGHTS

TRAVEL JOURNAL

MEMORIES AND PHOTOS

This Trip was...

MY CAMPING TRAVEL PLAN

Date: ______________

TRAVEL DIARY

S S M T W T F

Date:

Travel from :

Travel to :

Travel To-do List

Today's Expenses

Today's Travel Info

BEGINING MILEAGE

ENDING MILEAGE

MILES TRAVELLED

COST

FUEL

TRAVEL TIME

WEATHER

TEMPERATURE

Note:

CAMPGROUND DETAILS

TRAVEL ITINERARY

Date: ______________

S S M T W T F

AMENITIES	✓
WATER	○
ELECTRIC	○
SEWER	○
BACK IN	○
PULL THROUGH	○
SUN	○
SHADE	○
LEVEL	○
SLOPE	○
PAVED	○
PICNIC TABLE	○
FIRE PIT	○
WIFI	○
STORE	○
POOL	○
RESTROOMS	○
CLEAN	○
PET FRIENDLY	○
KID FRIENDLY	○

ACCOMODATION

Campground Name

Location:

Phone #

Site #

Cost $

# of Days staying

Site I Would Stay next time

____

Cell service ____________________

Notes ____________________

____

☆☆☆☆☆ Rating

PRIVACY	○
QUITE	○
NOISY	○
GRASS	○
GRAVEL	○

PLACES TO VISIT

THINGS TO DO

PLACES TO SEE

TRAILS, HIKING & BIKING

FOOD, DINING &RESTAURANTS

THINGS TO DO NEXT TIME

PEOPLE WE MET

HIGHLIGHTS

TRAVEL JOURNAL

MEMORIES AND PHOTOS

This Trip was...

MY CAMPING TRAVEL PLAN

Date: ______________

TRAVEL DIARY

S S M T W T F

Date:

Travel from :

Travel to :

Travel To-do List

Today's Expenses

Today's Travel Info

BEGINING MILEAGE

ENDING MILEAGE

MILES TRAVELLED

COST

FUEL

TRAVEL TIME

WEATHER

TEMPERATURE

Note:

CAMPGROUND DETAILS

TRAVEL ITINERARY

Date: ______________

S S M T W T F

AMENITIES	✓
WATER	○
ELECTRIC	○
SEWER	○
BACK IN	○
PULL THROUGH	○
SUN	○
SHADE	○
LEVEL	○
SLOPE	○
PAVED	○
PICNIC TABLE	○
FIRE PIT	○
WIFI	○
STORE	○
POOL	○
RESTROOMS	○
CLEAN	○
PET FRIENDLY	○
KID FRIENDLY	○

ACCOMODATION

Campground Name

Location:

Phone #

Site #

Cost $

# of Days staying

Site I Would Stay next time

____

Cell service ______________________

Notes ______________________

____

☆☆☆☆☆ Rating

PRIVACY	○
QUITE	○
NOISY	○
GRASS	○
GRAVEL	○

PLACES TO VISIT

THINGS TO DO

PLACES TO SEE

TRAILS, HIKING & BIKING

FOOD, DINING &RESTAURANTS

THINGS TO DO NEXT TIME

PEOPLE WE MET

HIGHLIGHTS

TRAVEL JOURNAL

MEMORIES AND PHOTOS

This Trip was...

MY CAMPING TRAVEL PLAN

Date: ______________

TRAVEL DIARY

S S M T W T F

Date:

Travel from :

Travel to :

Travel To-do List

Today's Expenses

Today's Travel Info

BEGINING MILEAGE

ENDING MILEAGE

MILES TRAVELLED

COST

FUEL

TRAVEL TIME

WEATHER

TEMPERATURE

Note:

CAMPGROUND DETAILS

TRAVEL ITINERARY

Date: ______________

S S M T W T F

AMENITIES	✓
WATER	○
ELECTRIC	○
SEWER	○
BACK IN	○
PULL THROUGH	○
SUN	○
SHADE	○
LEVEL	○
SLOPE	○
PAVED	○
PICNIC TABLE	○
FIRE PIT	○
WIFI	○
STORE	○
POOL	○
RESTROOMS	○
CLEAN	○
PET FRIENDLY	○
KID FRIENDLY	○

ACCOMODATION

Campground Name

Location:

Phone #

Site #

Cost $

# of Days staying

Site I Would Stay next time

____

Cell service ______________________

Notes ______________________

____

☆☆☆☆☆ Rating

PRIVACY	○
QUITE	○
NOISY	○
GRASS	○
GRAVEL	○

PLACES TO VISIT

THINGS TO DO

PLACES TO SEE

TRAILS, HIKING & BIKING

FOOD, DINING &RESTAURANTS

THINGS TO DO NEXT TIME

PEOPLE WE MET

HIGHLIGHTS

TRAVEL JOURNAL

MEMORIES AND PHOTOS

This Trip was...

MY CAMPING TRAVEL PLAN

Date: --------------

TRAVEL DIARY

S S M T W T F

Date:

Travel from :

Travel to :

Travel To-do List

Today's Travel Info

BEGINING MILEAGE

ENDING MILEAGE

MILES TRAVELLED

COST

FUEL

TRAVEL TIME

WEATHER

TEMPERATURE

Today's Expenses

Note:

CAMPGROUND DETAILS

TRAVEL ITINERARY

Date: --------------

S S M T W T F

AMENITIES	✓
WATER	○
ELECTRIC	○
SEWER	○
BACK IN	○
PULL THROUGH	○
SUN	○
SHADE	○
LEVEL	○
SLOPE	○
PAVED	○
PICNIC TABLE	○
FIRE PIT	○
WIFI	○
STORE	○
POOL	○
RESTROOMS	○
CLEAN	○
PET FRIENDLY	○
KID FRIENDLY	○

ACCOMODATION

Campground Name

Location:

Phone #

Site #

Cost $

# of Days staying

Site I Would Stay next time

____

Cell service ____________________

Notes __________________________

____

☆☆☆☆☆ Rating

PRIVACY	○
QUITE	○
NOISY	○
GRASS	○
GRAVEL	○

PLACES TO VISIT

THINGS TO DO

PLACES TO SEE

TRAILS, HIKING & BIKING

FOOD, DINING &RESTAURANTS

THINGS TO DO NEXT TIME

PEOPLE WE MET

HIGHLIGHTS

TRAVEL JOURNAL

MEMORIES AND PHOTOS

This Trip was...

MY CAMPING TRAVEL PLAN

Date: --------------

TRAVEL DIARY

S S M T W T F

Date:

Travel from :

Travel to :

Travel To-do List

Today's Expenses

Today's Travel Info

BEGINING MILEAGE

ENDING MILEAGE

MILES TRAVELLED

COST

FUEL

TRAVEL TIME

WEATHER

TEMPERATURE

Note:

CAMPGROUND DETAILS

TRAVEL ITINERARY

Date: ______________

S S M T W T F

AMENITIES	✓
WATER	○
ELECTRIC	○
SEWER	○
BACK IN	○
PULL THROUGH	○
SUN	○
SHADE	○
LEVEL	○
SLOPE	○
PAVED	○
PICNIC TABLE	○
FIRE PIT	○
WIFI	○
STORE	○
POOL	○
RESTROOMS	○
CLEAN	○
PET FRIENDLY	○
KID FRIENDLY	○

ACCOMODATION

Campground Name

Location:

Phone #

Site #

Cost $

# of Days staying

Site I Would Stay next time

____

Cell service ______________

Notes ______________________

____

☆☆☆☆☆ Rating

PRIVACY	○
QUITE	○
NOISY	○
GRASS	○
GRAVEL	○

PLACES TO VISIT

THINGS TO DO

PLACES TO SEE

TRAILS, HIKING & BIKING

FOOD, DINING &RESTAURANTS

THINGS TO DO NEXT TIME

PEOPLE WE MET

HIGHLIGHTS

TRAVEL JOURNAL

MEMORIES AND PHOTOS

This Trip was...

MY CAMPING TRAVEL PLAN

Date: --------------

TRAVEL DIARY

S S M T W T F

Date:

Travel from :

Travel to :

Travel To-do List

Today's Expenses

Today's Travel Info

BEGINING MILEAGE

ENDING MILEAGE

MILES TRAVELLED

COST

FUEL

TRAVEL TIME

WEATHER

TEMPERATURE

Note:

CAMPGROUND DETAILS

TRAVEL ITINERARY

Date: ______________

S S M T W T F

AMENITIES	✓
WATER	○
ELECTRIC	○
SEWER	○
BACK IN	○
PULL THROUGH	○
SUN	○
SHADE	○
LEVEL	○
SLOPE	○
PAVED	○
PICNIC TABLE	○
FIRE PIT	○
WIFI	○
STORE	○
POOL	○
RESTROOMS	○
CLEAN	○
PET FRIENDLY	○
KID FRIENDLY	○

ACCOMODATION

Campground Name

Location:

Phone #

Site #

Cost $

# of Days staying

Site I Would Stay next time

____

Cell service _______________

Notes _______________

____

☆☆☆☆☆ Rating

PRIVACY	○
QUITE	○
NOISY	○
GRASS	○
GRAVEL	○

PLACES TO VISIT

THINGS TO DO

PLACES TO SEE

TRAILS, HIKING & BIKING

FOOD, DINING &RESTAURANTS

THINGS TO DO NEXT TIME

PEOPLE WE MET

HIGHLIGHTS

TRAVEL JOURNAL

MEMORIES AND PHOTOS

This Trip was...

MY CAMPING TRAVEL PLAN

Date: --------------

TRAVEL DIARY

S S M T W T F

Date:

Travel from :

Travel to :

Travel To-do List

Today's Expenses

Today's Travel Info

BEGINING MILEAGE

ENDING MILEAGE

MILES TRAVELLED

COST

FUEL

TRAVEL TIME

WEATHER

TEMPERATURE

Note:

CAMPGROUND DETAILS

TRAVEL ITINERARY

Date: ______________

S S M T W T F

AMENITIES	✓
WATER	○
ELECTRIC	○
SEWER	○
BACK IN	○
PULL THROUGH	○
SUN	○
SHADE	○
LEVEL	○
SLOPE	○
PAVED	○
PICNIC TABLE	○
FIRE PIT	○
WIFI	○
STORE	○
POOL	○
RESTROOMS	○
CLEAN	○
PET FRIENDLY	○
KID FRIENDLY	○

ACCOMODATION
Campground Name
Location:
Phone #
Site #
Cost $
# of Days staying

Site I Would Stay next time

____

Cell service ______________________

Notes ______________________________

____

☆☆☆☆☆ Rating

PRIVACY	○
QUITE	○
NOISY	○
GRASS	○
GRAVEL	○

PLACES TO VISIT

THINGS TO DO

PLACES TO SEE

TRAILS, HIKING & BIKING

FOOD, DINING &RESTAURANTS

THINGS TO DO NEXT TIME

PEOPLE WE MET

HIGHLIGHTS

TRAVEL JOURNAL

MEMORIES AND PHOTOS

This Trip was...

MY CAMPING TRAVEL PLAN

Date: --------------

TRAVEL DIARY

S S M T W T F

Date:

Travel from :

Travel to :

Travel To-do List

Today's Travel Info

BEGINING MILEAGE

ENDING MILEAGE

MILES TRAVELLED

COST

FUEL

TRAVEL TIME

WEATHER

TEMPERATURE

Today's Expenses

Note:

CAMPGROUND DETAILS

Date: _______________

TRAVEL ITINERARY

S S M T W T F

AMENITIES	✓
WATER	○
ELECTRIC	○
SEWER	○
BACK IN	○
PULL THROUGH	○
SUN	○
SHADE	○
LEVEL	○
SLOPE	○
PAVED	○
PICNIC TABLE	○
FIRE PIT	○
WIFI	○
STORE	○
POOL	○
RESTROOMS	○
CLEAN	○
PET FRIENDLY	○
KID FRIENDLY	○

ACCOMODATION

Campground Name

Location:

Phone #

Site #

Cost $

# of Days staying

Site I Would Stay next time

____

Cell service _______________

Notes _______________

____

☆☆☆☆☆ Rating

PRIVACY	○
QUITE	○
NOISY	○
GRASS	○
GRAVEL	○

PLACES TO VISIT

THINGS TO DO

PLACES TO SEE

TRAILS, HIKING & BIKING

FOOD, DINING &RESTAURANTS

THINGS TO DO NEXT TIME

PEOPLE WE MET

HIGHLIGHTS

TRAVEL JOURNAL

MEMORIES AND PHOTOS

This Trip was...

MY CAMPING TRAVEL PLAN

Date: --------------

TRAVEL DIARY

S S M T W T F

Date:

Travel from :

Travel to :

Travel To-do List

Today's Expenses

Today's Travel Info

BEGINING MILEAGE

ENDING MILEAGE

MILES TRAVELLED

COST

FUEL

TRAVEL TIME

WEATHER

TEMPERATURE

Note:

CAMPGROUND DETAILS

Date: ______________

TRAVEL ITINERARY

S S M T W T F

AMENITIES	✓
WATER	○
ELECTRIC	○
SEWER	○
BACK IN	○
PULL THROUGH	○
SUN	○
SHADE	○
LEVEL	○
SLOPE	○
PAVED	○
PICNIC TABLE	○
FIRE PIT	○
WIFI	○
STORE	○
POOL	○
RESTROOMS	○
CLEAN	○
PET FRIENDLY	○
KID FRIENDLY	○

ACCOMODATION

Campground Name

Location:

Phone #

Site #

Cost $

# of Days staying

Site I Would Stay next time

____

Cell service ____________________

Notes ____________________

____

☆☆☆☆☆ Rating

PRIVACY	○
QUITE	○
NOISY	○
GRASS	○
GRAVEL	○

PLACES TO VISIT

THINGS TO DO

PLACES TO SEE

TRAILS, HIKING & BIKING

FOOD, DINING &RESTAURANTS

THINGS TO DO NEXT TIME

PEOPLE WE MET

HIGHLIGHTS

TRAVEL JOURNAL

MEMORIES AND PHOTOS

This Trip was...

MY CAMPING TRAVEL PLAN

Date: --------------

TRAVEL DIARY

S S M T W T F

Date:

Travel from :

Travel to :

Travel To-do List

Today's Expenses

Today's Travel Info

BEGINING MILEAGE

ENDING MILEAGE

MILES TRAVELLED

COST

FUEL

TRAVEL TIME

WEATHER

TEMPERATURE

Note:

CAMPGROUND DETAILS

TRAVEL ITINERARY

Date: ______________

S S M T W T F

AMENITIES	✓
WATER	○
ELECTRIC	○
SEWER	○
BACK IN	○
PULL THROUGH	○
SUN	○
SHADE	○
LEVEL	○
SLOPE	○
PAVED	○
PICNIC TABLE	○
FIRE PIT	○
WIFI	○
STORE	○
POOL	○
RESTROOMS	○
CLEAN	○
PET FRIENDLY	○
KID FRIENDLY	○

ACCOMODATION

Campground Name

Location:

Phone #

Site #

Cost $

# of Days staying

Site I Would Stay next time

____

Cell service ______________________

Notes ______________________

____

☆☆☆☆☆ Rating

PRIVACY	○
QUITE	○
NOISY	○
GRASS	○
GRAVEL	○

PLACES TO VISIT

THINGS TO DO

PLACES TO SEE

TRAILS, HIKING & BIKING

FOOD, DINING &RESTAURANTS

THINGS TO DO NEXT TIME

PEOPLE WE MET

HIGHLIGHTS

TRAVEL JOURNAL

MEMORIES AND PHOTOS

This Trip was...

MY CAMPING TRAVEL PLAN

Date: --------------

TRAVEL DIARY

S S M T W T F

Date:

Travel from :

Travel to :

Travel To-do List

Today's Expenses

Today's Travel Info

BEGINING MILEAGE

ENDING MILEAGE

MILES TRAVELLED

COST

FUEL

TRAVEL TIME

WEATHER

TEMPERATURE

Note:

CAMPGROUND DETAILS

TRAVEL ITINERARY

Date: ______________

S S M T W T F

AMENITIES	✓
WATER	○
ELECTRIC	○
SEWER	○
BACK IN	○
PULL THROUGH	○
SUN	○
SHADE	○
LEVEL	○
SLOPE	○
PAVED	○
PICNIC TABLE	○
FIRE PIT	○
WIFI	○
STORE	○
POOL	○
RESTROOMS	○
CLEAN	○
PET FRIENDLY	○
KID FRIENDLY	○

ACCOMODATION

Campground Name

Location:

Phone #

Site #

Cost $

# of Days staying

Site I Would Stay next time

____

Cell service ______________________

Notes ______________________

____

☆☆☆☆☆ Rating

PRIVACY	○
QUITE	○
NOISY	○
GRASS	○
GRAVEL	○

PLACES TO VISIT

THINGS TO DO

PLACES TO SEE

TRAILS, HIKING & BIKING

FOOD, DINING &RESTAURANTS

THINGS TO DO NEXT TIME

PEOPLE WE MET

HIGHLIGHTS

TRAVEL JOURNAL

MEMORIES AND PHOTOS

This Trip was...

MY CAMPING TRAVEL PLAN

Date: ______________

TRAVEL DIARY

S S M T W T F

Date:

Travel from :

Travel to :

Travel To-do List

Today's Expenses

Today's Travel Info

BEGINING MILEAGE

ENDING MILEAGE

MILES TRAVELLED

COST

FUEL

TRAVEL TIME

WEATHER

TEMPERATURE

Note:

CAMPGROUND DETAILS

Date: ______________

TRAVEL ITINERARY

S S M T W T F

AMENITIES	✓
WATER	○
ELECTRIC	○
SEWER	○
BACK IN	○
PULL THROUGH	○
SUN	○
SHADE	○
LEVEL	○
SLOPE	○
PAVED	○
PICNIC TABLE	○
FIRE PIT	○
WIFI	○
STORE	○
POOL	○
RESTROOMS	○
CLEAN	○
PET FRIENDLY	○
KID FRIENDLY	○

ACCOMODATION

Campground Name

Location:

Phone #

Site #

Cost $

# of Days staying

Site I Would Stay next time

____

Cell service ______________________

Notes ______________________

____

☆☆☆☆☆ Rating

PRIVACY	○
QUITE	○
NOISY	○
GRASS	○
GRAVEL	○

PLACES TO VISIT

THINGS TO DO

PLACES TO SEE

TRAILS, HIKING & BIKING

FOOD, DINING &RESTAURANTS

THINGS TO DO NEXT TIME

PEOPLE WE MET

HIGHLIGHTS

TRAVEL JOURNAL

MEMORIES AND PHOTOS

This Trip was...

MY CAMPING TRAVEL PLAN

Date: ______________

TRAVEL DIARY

S S M T W T F

Date:

Travel from :

Travel to :

Travel To-do List

Today's Expenses

Today's Travel Info

BEGINING MILEAGE

ENDING MILEAGE

MILES TRAVELLED

COST

FUEL

TRAVEL TIME

WEATHER

TEMPERATURE

Note:

CAMPGROUND DETAILS

Date: ______________

TRAVEL ITINERARY

S S M T W T F

AMENITIES	✔
WATER	○
ELECTRIC	○
SEWER	○
BACK IN	○
PULL THROUGH	○
SUN	○
SHADE	○
LEVEL	○
SLOPE	○
PAVED	○
PICNIC TABLE	○
FIRE PIT	○
WIFI	○
STORE	○
POOL	○
RESTROOMS	○
CLEAN	○
PET FRIENDLY	○
KID FRIENDLY	○

ACCOMODATION

Campground Name

Location:

Phone #

Site #

Cost $

# of Days staying

Site I Would Stay next time

____

Cell service ______________

Notes ______________

____

☆☆☆☆☆ Rating

PRIVACY	○
QUITE	○
NOISY	○
GRASS	○
GRAVEL	○

PLACES TO VISIT

THINGS TO DO

PLACES TO SEE

TRAILS, HIKING & BIKING

FOOD, DINING &RESTAURANTS

THINGS TO DO NEXT TIME

PEOPLE WE MET

HIGHLIGHTS

TRAVEL JOURNAL

MEMORIES AND PHOTOS

This Trip was...

MY CAMPING TRAVEL PLAN

Date: --------------

TRAVEL DIARY

S S M T W T F

Date:

Travel from :

Travel to :

Travel To-do List

Today's Expenses

Today's Travel Info

BEGINING MILEAGE

ENDING MILEAGE

MILES TRAVELLED

COST

FUEL

TRAVEL TIME

WEATHER

TEMPERATURE

Note:

CAMPGROUND DETAILS

Date: --------------

TRAVEL ITINERARY

S S M T W T F

AMENITIES	✓
WATER	○
ELECTRIC	○
SEWER	○
BACK IN	○
PULL THROUGH	○
SUN	○
SHADE	○
LEVEL	○
SLOPE	○
PAVED	○
PICNIC TABLE	○
FIRE PIT	○
WIFI	○
STORE	○
POOL	○
RESTROOMS	○
CLEAN	○
PET FRIENDLY	○
KID FRIENDLY	○

ACCOMODATION

Campground Name

Location:

Phone #

Site #

Cost $

# of Days staying

Site I Would Stay next time

____

Cell service ______________________

Notes ______________________

____

☆☆☆☆☆ Rating

PRIVACY	○
QUITE	○
NOISY	○
GRASS	○
GRAVEL	○

PLACES TO VISIT

THINGS TO DO

PLACES TO SEE

TRAILS, HIKING & BIKING

FOOD, DINING &RESTAURANTS

THINGS TO DO NEXT TIME

PEOPLE WE MET

HIGHLIGHTS

TRAVEL JOURNAL

MEMORIES AND PHOTOS

This Trip was...

MY CAMPING TRAVEL PLAN

Date: ______________

TRAVEL DIARY

S S M T W T F

Date:

Travel from :

Travel to :

Travel To-do List

Today's Expenses

Today's Travel Info

BEGINING MILEAGE

ENDING MILEAGE

MILES TRAVELLED

COST

FUEL

TRAVEL TIME

WEATHER

TEMPERATURE

Note:

CAMPGROUND DETAILS

TRAVEL ITINERARY

Date: --------------

S S M T W T F

AMENITIES	✓
WATER	○
ELECTRIC	○
SEWER	○
BACK IN	○
PULL THROUGH	○
SUN	○
SHADE	○
LEVEL	○
SLOPE	○
PAVED	○
PICNIC TABLE	○
FIRE PIT	○
WIFI	○
STORE	○
POOL	○
RESTROOMS	○
CLEAN	○
PET FRIENDLY	○
KID FRIENDLY	○

ACCOMODATION

Campground Name

Location:

Phone #

Site #

Cost $

# of Days staying

Site I Would Stay next time

____

Cell service ____________________

Notes ______________________

____

☆☆☆☆☆ Rating

PRIVACY	○
QUITE	○
NOISY	○
GRASS	○
GRAVEL	○

PLACES TO VISIT

THINGS TO DO

PLACES TO SEE

TRAILS, HIKING & BIKING

FOOD, DINING &RESTAURANTS

THINGS TO DO NEXT TIME

PEOPLE WE MET

HIGHLIGHTS

TRAVEL JOURNAL

MEMORIES AND PHOTOS

This Trip was...

FAVOURITE MEMORIES THIS YEAR

TRAVEL REVIEW

This Year was the Best ...

FAVOURITE MEMORIES THIS YEAR

TRAVEL REVIEW

This Year was the Best ...

FAVOURITE MEMORIES THIS YEAR

TRAVEL REVIEW

This Year was the Best ...

Made in the USA
Middletown, DE
30 May 2023